21st Century Junior Library

Screwdrivers

by Josh Gregory

CHERRY LAKE PUBLISHING * ANN ARBOR, MICHIGAN

Published in the United States of America by Cherry Lake Publishing
Ann Arbor, Michigan
www.cherrylakepublishing.com

Content Adviser: Roger McGregor, Director, Hannibal Career & Technical Center, Hannibal, Missouri

Reading Adviser: Marla Conn, ReadAbility, Inc.

Photo Credits: Cover, ©iStockphoto.com/fstop123; page 4, ©iStockphoto.com/Zmiy; page 6, ©Ingvar Bjork/Shutterstock, Inc.; page 8, ©Lasse Kristensen/Shutterstock, Inc.; page 10, ©Ilya Shapovalov/Shutterstock, Inc.; page 12, ©iStockphoto.com/clausjepsen; page 14, ©auremar/Shutterstock, Inc.; page 16, ©Steve Collender/Shutterstock, Inc.; page 18, © kilukilu/Shutterstock, Inc.; page 20, ©iStockphoto.com/bezmaski.

LIBRARY OF CONGRESS CATALOGING-IN-PUBLICATION DATA
Gregory, Josh
  Screwdrivers/by Josh Gregory
      pages cm.—(Basic tools) (21st century junior library)
  Audience: K to grade 3.
  Includes bibliographical references and index.
  ISBN 978-1-62431-169-7 (library binding)—ISBN 978-1-62431-301-1 (paperback)—
ISBN 978-1-62431-235-9 (e-book)
  1. Screwdrivers—Juvenile literature. I. Title. II. Title: Screwdrivers.
  TJ1201.S34G74 2013
  621.9'72—dc23   2013004932

*Cherry Lake Publishing would like to acknowledge the work of
The Partnership for 21st Century Skills.
Please visit www.p21.org for more information.*

Printed in the United States of America
Corporate Graphics Inc.
July 2013
CLFA13

CONTENTS

5 What Is a Screwdriver?

11 How Are Screwdrivers Used?

17 Different Kinds of Screwdrivers

22 Glossary

23 Find Out More

24 Index

24 About the Author

Working on computers and other devices often requires very small screwdrivers.

What Is a Screwdriver?

Have you seen someone working on the inside of a computer? Maybe you have watched a person put together a shelf or table. If so, you have probably seen someone using a screwdriver.

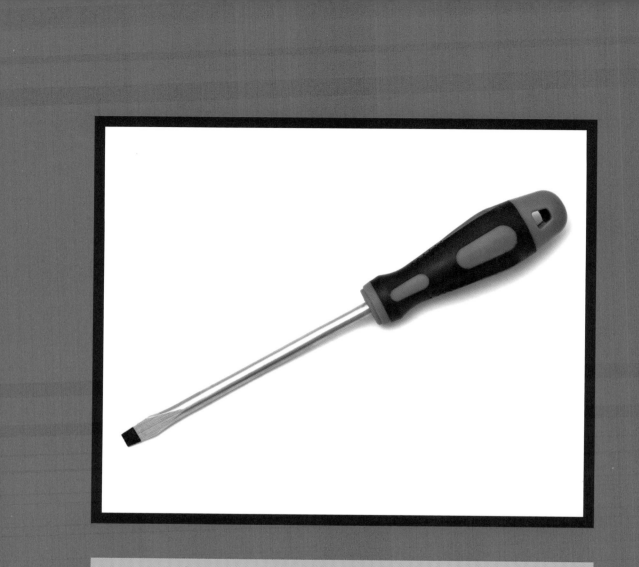

Screwdriver handles are usually shaped so that a person can hold them comfortably.

A screwdriver usually has a long **shank**. A pointed tip is at one end. A handle is at the other end. The shank and the tip are made of strong metal. The handle can be made of wood, metal, or plastic. Sometimes it is coated in rubber. This keeps it from slipping out of a person's hand.

Screws come in many different shapes and sizes.

Screwdrivers are not very useful without screws. Screws are pieces of metal used to hold things together. One end of a screw is pointed. The other end is called the **head**. It has a slot on top. A spiral shape is between the head and tip. This is called a **thread**.

Look!

Take a look at some objects in your house. Are any of them held together using screws? What do you notice about the screw heads you see? How are they alike or different?

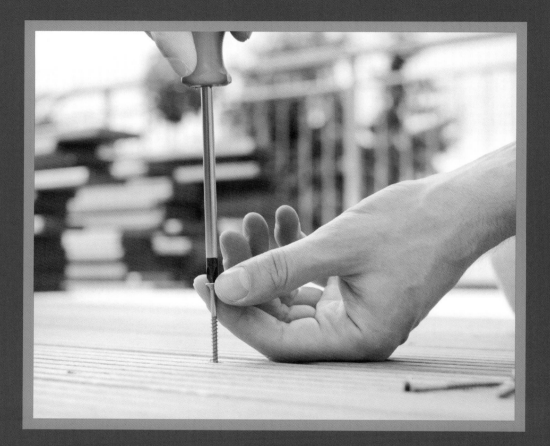

Turning a screw clockwise, or to the right, tightens it. Turning it to the left loosens it.

How Are Screwdrivers Used?

A worker puts a screw's pointed end into a hole. The screwdriver tip fits into the slot on the screw head. Then the worker turns the screwdriver's handle. This twists the screw's thread into the hole.

People use power drills to quickly create holes for screws.

Screws go into holes that were made ahead of time. Sometimes people use a **drill** to create the holes. This works best when using screws in wood. A screw's thread digs into a hole's sides as the screw twists. This keeps the screw from being pulled out.

Make a Guess!

Why are screws sometimes used instead of nails? Is one better at holding certain things together? Think about the way screw threads work.

The pieces used to make an electric outlet come with premade holes. This makes it easier for electricians to put the pieces together.

Sometimes, screws hold pieces of metal or plastic together. The pieces usually come with holes already in them. These holes have their own threads inside. This is because a screw's thread cannot dig into the metal. The screw's thread fits into the thread in the hole.

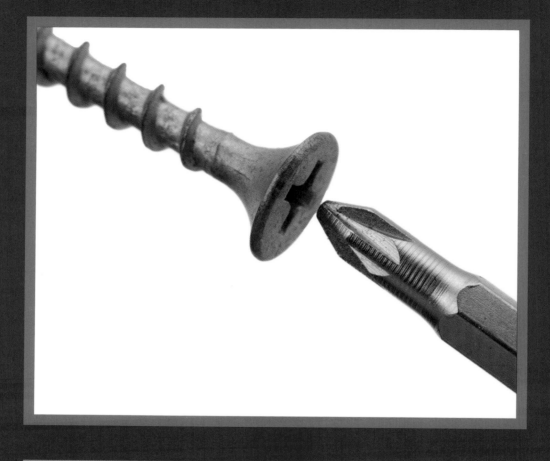

This Phillips screwdriver matches the cross shape cut into the screw head.

Different Kinds of Screwdrivers

Different screws have different slots in their heads. Some have a single line cut into them. These screws need a screwdriver with a flat blade tip. Others have a cross-shaped slot in the head. These screws need a Phillips head screwdriver. Some have square and star-shaped slots. These need special screwdrivers.

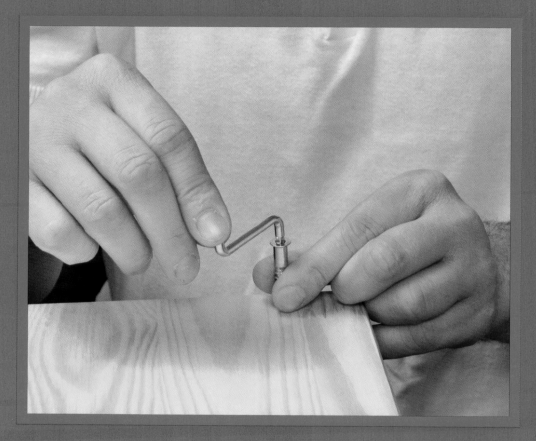

Offset screwdrivers are often used when people put furniture together.

Some screwdrivers have different shapes. This can help workers reach difficult spots. A screwdriver's handle might stick out to the side. This lets a worker drive screws in deep and narrow holes. The screwdriver can reach places a worker's hands cannot.

Electric screwdrivers sometimes look similar to power drills.

Some screwdrivers are powered by electricity. A worker simply presses a button. This turns the screwdriver. Electric screwdrivers make it easier and faster to drive in screws.

Keep an eye out for screws in objects you use. You never know where you will find one of these fasteners!

Create!

Try using a screwdriver at home. Ask your parents if you can take apart a simple toy. Pay careful attention to how all the parts fit together. You need to remember how to put them back together afterward!

GLOSSARY

drill (DRIL) a tool used for making holes

head (HED) the flat end of a screw

shank (SHAYNK) the long rod that connects a screwdriver's handle to its tip

thread (THRED) the raised lines that wind around the side of a screw

FIND OUT MORE

BOOKS

Hanson, Anders. *Screwdrivers.* Edina, MN: ABDO, 2010.

Nelson, Robin. *What Does a Screwdriver Do?* Minneapolis: Lerner, 2013.

WEB SITES

How It's Made: Screwdrivers

http://science.discovery.com /tv-shows/how-its-made/videos/how -its-made-screwdrivers.htm
Watch a video that shows how screwdrivers are made.

History of Screws and Screwdrivers

http://inventors.about.com/od /sstartinventions/a/screwdriver.htm
Learn more about the history of screwdrivers.

INDEX

D
drills, 13

E
electric screwdrivers,
   21

H
handles, 7, 11, 19
heads, 9, 11, 17
holes, 11, 13, 15, 19

M
metal, 7, 9, 15

N
nails, 13

P
Phillips head
   screwdrivers, 17
plastic, 7, 15

R
rubber, 7

S
screws, 9, 11, 13,
   15, 17, 19, 21
shanks, 7

shapes, 9, 17, 19
slots, 9, 11, 17

T
threads, 9, 11, 13, 15
tips, 7, 9, 11, 17

W
wood, 7, 13
workers, 5, 7, 11, 13,
   19, 21

ABOUT THE AUTHOR

Josh Gregory writes and edits books for kids. He lives in Chicago, Illinois.